*This book is dedicated to Susan Margaret Gray,
who taught me to dance* –L. S.

For Eleanor –J. M.

Special thanks to Ilsa Bush
for her generous consultation in the making of this book.

Library of Congress Cataloging-in-Publication Data:
Snyder, Laurel.
Swan : the life and dance of Anna Pavlova / by Laurel Snyder;
illustrated by Julie Morstad.
pages cm
ISBN 978-1-4521-1890-1 (alk. paper)
1. Pavlova, Anna, 1881-1931—Juvenile literature.
2. Ballerinas—Russia (Federation)—Biography—Juvenile literature. I. Title.

GV1785.P3S69 2015
792.802'8092—dc23
[B]

2013013706

Manufactured in China.

Design by Kristine Brogno.
Typeset in Cabrito.
The illustrations in this book were rendered in ink,
gouache, graphite, pencil, and crayon.

10 9 8 7 6 5 4 3 2 1

Chronicle Books LLC
680 Second Street, San Francisco, California 94107

Chronicle Books—we see things differently.
Become part of our community at www.chroniclekids.com.

Swan

The LIFE and DANCE
of ANNA PAVLOVA

by LAUREL SNYDER   illustrated by JULIE MORSTAD

chronicle books · san francisco

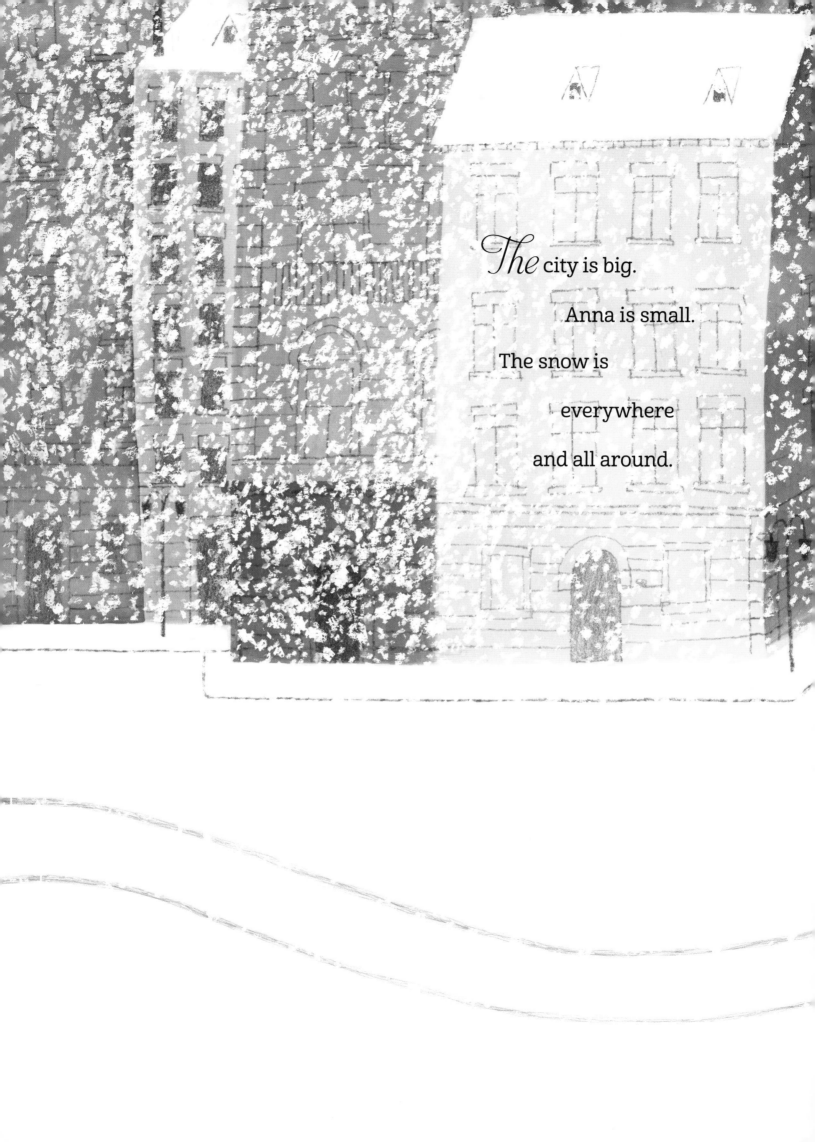

The city is big.

Anna is small.

The snow is

everywhere

and all around.

But one night . . .

Anna's sleigh

slips up the street.

Her face is cold.

The world is dark.

Mama smiles.

Then—ah!

The lights.

The lights!

Something is happening . . .

There's a swell of strings,

a scurry of skirts.

A hiss and a hum and . . .

HUSH!

It's
all
beginning!

The story unfolds. A sleeping beauty opens her eyes

. . . and so does Anna.

Her feet wake up!

Her skin prickles.

There is a song, suddenly, inside her.

Now Anna cannot sleep.

Or sit

still

ever.

She can only sway,
    dip, and spin. . . .

Now Mama hums into her soup.

Now the snow skitters
    just so at the window.

Now the squirrels stop to watch.

At last Mama nods, and out of her house
Anna goes, into the world of people.

Tall people.

And oh?

Oh.

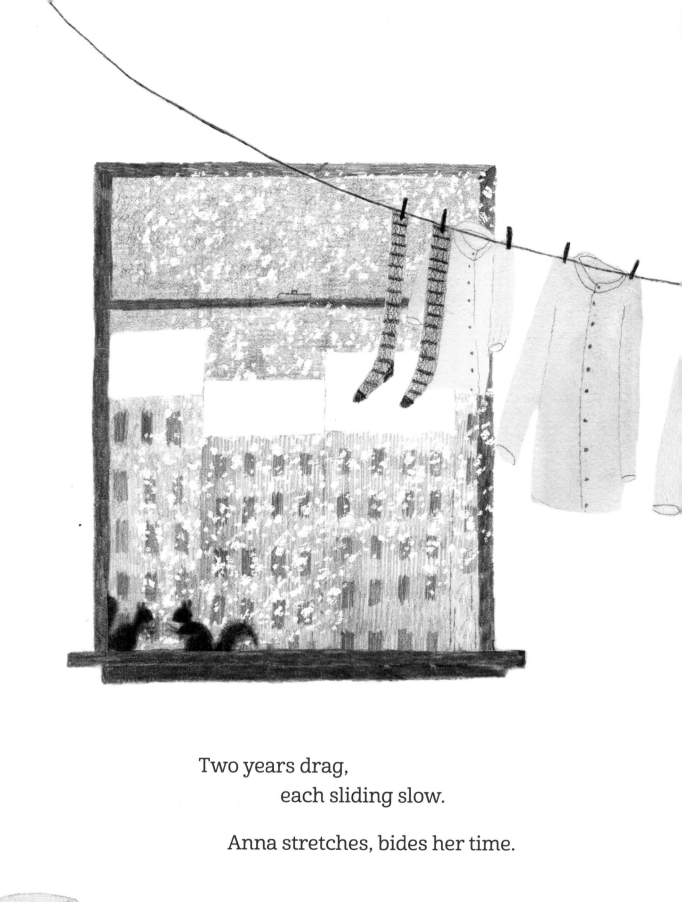

Two years drag,
        each sliding slow.

Anna stretches, bides her time.

Shirt, shirt, *laundry.*
Shirt, shirt, *laundry.*

Even the squirrels lose interest.

But *this* time, oh?

Oh yes!

The work begins.

The work?

The work!

Up

and down

and to and fro

and third position!

and back and turn

and on and on

Again!

Again!

Again!

Until one night
she takes the stage . . .

Anna becomes

a glimmer, a grace.

Everyone feels it,

and the lamps shine brighter.

The room holds its breath.

It shouldn't be that she should be

this good.

Her legs too thin,
her feet all wrong—

and ooh, those toes!

She is only a girl—
so small—so frail—

but

see her face, her flutter?

Anna was born for this.

For five bright years

the dancers swirl around Anna.

The curtains rise and fall.

Finally,

she steps onto the stage alone . . .

and sprouts white wings, a swan.

She weaves the notes, the very air

into a story.

All those sitting see.

They stare—

Anna is a bird in flight,
a whim of wind and water.

Quiet feathers in a big loud world.

Anna *is* the swan.

Across the globe she sails.

There are furs and riches.

Kings and Queens.

Pearls to be worn.

Toasts to be drunk.

But it is not enough.

Anna remembers a small cold room,

a lonely girl at a window.

Shirt, shirt, *laundry.*
Shirt, shirt, *laundry.*

Somewhere, there are people who haven't heard the music.

Anna sails on.

Forests and plains,

sprawling cities and tiny towns.

The world is a hungry place,

and Anna will feed it beauty.

Across bullrings and the warped boards of dance halls,

she moves

everyone.

The sick and the poor

come to meet her boats and trains, they cheer her,

and are cheered.

Anna walks in the rain, sleeps on the floor.

She is—a queen,

a dragonfly!

a ghost,

a bit of snow,

And again and again   and best of all,   the swan.

When people throw flowers, Anna tosses them back.

It's enough just to dance.

Of course, always the tour ends, the boat docks,
                    the train returns to the station . . .

        and there are
                    pets and people,
        meals and meetings,
                    hearth and home.

    But not the home Anna remembers . . .

            home is gone.

    Anna won't return to the snowy city.

        There has been a war there, a wall.
                        Everything is changed.

    Sleighs no longer jingle
            through the streets of Petrograd.

Anna builds a new life,
a different fairy tale.

Until a chill finds Anna, hunts her down, alone,

without her boots and mittens.

A wind. A cough beside a stopped train.

A rattle she can't shake.

Anna tries to waltz away, to spin and sway.

She'll turn and turn and turn from this, she thinks.

If she can just keep dancing.

She calls for her feathers.

But . . .

Every day must end in night.

Every bird must fold its wings.

Every feather falls at last, and settles.

Oh, thinks Anna.

If only every dance could end

in such

sweet

applause.

From the Author

Anna Pavlova was born in 1881 to a struggling laundress. It was a hard life, and Russia under the czars was generally a world where the poor stayed poor. Anna's life *should* have been dismal.

But one night Anna's mother told her, "You are going to enter fairyland," as the two climbed into their sleigh and sped off to the Mariinsky Theatre. There, Anna heard Tchaikovsky's music for the first time. She watched the dancers step out onto the stage, and her life was changed forever. Anna knew what she wanted to do with her life.

"In order to become a dancer," her mother warned her, "you will have to leave your mother and become a pupil of the ballet school. My little Nura would not like to forsake her mama, would she?" In Russia in those days, ballerinas were trained at boarding schools, and Anna had never been away from her mother.

But Anna's hunger to dance was fierce, so when she was eight, she auditioned for the Imperial Ballet School. She was turned away because she was still too young. She had to wait patiently for another two years.

When she was accepted at age ten, Anna discovered that while she was graceful and had a natural gift for dance, her body was far from ideal for ballet. Dancers of that time were sturdy and acrobatic. Anna was thin and frail, with a weak back and severely arched feet that made it difficult for her to go up *en pointe*. The other girls at the school made fun of her for being so thin, calling her nicknames like "the broom."

But Anna refused to let anything stop her. She worked hard, and reinforced her ballet shoes to help her stay up on her toes. (In fact, the shoes dancers wear today are modeled after the shoes Anna constructed for herself.) In the end, her frailty lent itself to a different sort of dance—a more dramatic, romantic, evocative style. Anna trembled and moved lightly. She danced the lead role in all the great ballets—*Giselle, Les Sylphides, The Sleeping Beauty*, and especially

The Dying Swan—as no one had seen them danced before. She went on to become a very famous ballerina. Many believe she was the greatest ballerina of all time.

But as extraordinary as she was as a dancer, Anna's real contribution was that she believed ballet was for everyone. At the beginning of the twentieth century, ballet was a European art form, and it belonged exclusively to the wealthy. But ballet had changed Anna's life, and she felt it could do the same for other people. She set out to share her art, traveling the world and performing in some very odd places—from bullfighting rings to the backs of elephants. She shared her gifts with the poor as well as the rich. She inspired people everywhere she went.

Then, in the winter of 1931, Anna's train collided with another and came to a sudden stop. She went outside and walked the length of the train in her pajamas to find out what had happened, but she caught a cold, which turned into a deadly pneumonia (or pleurisy, sources differ). Though she wanted to keep dancing, Anna was far too ill, and for the first time in her life, she had to miss a performance.

In her fever, she called for her swan dress, as though she might still perform. But it was not to be. Anna died that night. Her last words were "Play that last measure very softly."

When I think about Anna Pavlova, I think of her Swan. But much more than that, I think of all the girls and boys who love ballet. I think of all of us—millions of us, all over the world (me too!)—pulling on our ballet shoes, working at the barre, or spinning chaînés turns across the floor. All of us laboring in the smells of sweat and crushed rosin; all of us reaching for beauty. And indebted to Anna, who led the way.

Bibliography

Algeranoff, Harcourt. *My Years with Pavlova*. London: William Heinemann, 1957.

Allman, Barbara. *Dance of the Swan: A Story about Anna Pavlova*. Minneapolis: Lerner, 2001.

Dandré, Victor. *Anna Pavlova in Art & Life*. New York: Benjamin Blom, 1972.

DeMello, Margo. *Feet & Footwear: A Cultural Encyclopedia*. Portsmouth: Greenwood, 2009.

Fonteyn, Margot. *Pavlova: Portrait of a Dancer*. New York: Viking, 1984.

Homans, Jennifer. *Apollo's Angels: A History of Ballet*. New York: Random House, 2011.

Kerensky, Oleg. *Anna Pavlova*. New York: Dutton, 1973.

Levine, Ellen. *Anna Pavlova: Genius of the Dance*. New York: Scholastic, 1995.

Svetloff, V. *Anna Pavlova*. Translated by A. Grey. New York: Dover Publications, 1974.

Quotation Sources

Levine, Ellen. *Anna Pavlova: Genius of the Dance*. New York: Scholastic, 1995: p 115.

Svetloff, V. *Anna Pavlova*. Translated by A. Grey. New York: Dover Publications, 1974: pp 116, 117.